Any Psalm You Want
a collection of poetry

♋

by Khary Jackson

Write Bloody Publishing
America's Independent Press

Austin, TX

WRITEBLOODY.COM

Jackson, Khary.
1ª edition.
ISBN: 978-1938912-22-1

Interior Layout by Lea C. Deschenes
Cover Designed by Jennifer Heuer
Author Photo by Xena Goldman
Proofread by Jessica Standifird
Edited by Derrick Brown
Type set in Bergamo from www.theleagueofmoveabletype.com

The author would like to acknowledge:

My family. For making me and living with what I am.

Darci Schummer and Michael Mlekoday for helping me prepare this book for submission.

Cave Canem, for inspiring and shaping some of my favorite poems in this book.

Sheila and Ron. Blair. Twin Cities poetry family.

And for the following folks who chose to publish some of these poems: *The Legendary* (From Antonio), *Muzzle* (For Brenda Moossy), *Bestiary* (Rosa Parks), *Cave Canem* (Enactment).

Printed in Tennessee, USA
Write Bloody Publishing
Austin, TX
Support Independent Presses
writebloody.com

To contact the author, send an email to writebloody@gmail.com

MADE IN THE USA

ANY PSALM YOU WANT

Any Psalm You Want

ENACTMENT

A hundred years from now, Civil War re-enactments will
be dead. In their place: every Juneteenth, solemn young
hands will wrap red (or blue) bandanas around their heads,
warm up the low rider, polish off the AKs and .45s,
and cruise around the 'hood with Snoop (Doggy) Dogg on blast.
The faces of old black women will, on cue, peer through their
windows at the bobbing car, and upon seeing the boys and their guns and
their gyrating arms, the old black women will dive to the floor
and mouth a prayer to the Lawd. An unfortunate black boy
standing in the front yard, unable to escape in time, will twist
his torso, yank his limbs to the choreographed puncture
of lungs, thump the grass without bracing his fall. His eyes
will flicker shut. He will imagine he can no longer breathe.
And from somewhere near, from everywhere, a forty-year-old
black woman will howl for her boy. Her hands will shred the air.

At the corner, in the liquor store, the cashier is calmly shaking
his head, preparing to tell the first listener *that boy was*
a good boy. In the store is a forty-ounce bottle, waiting to be opened.
Waiting for its moment to dance the blood.

FOR BRENDA MOOSSY

She told me she'd distinguished the soul of a gator
by the taste of its spine, by how many taste buds
tore off upon it, ravenous. Then she laughed
until a nymph spat out.
I married the swamp for nothin' but her mania.
She said it's the closest we can come to your mouth,
begged me to one day bury her in the Ozarks.

Somewhere there's a licked-open cow gut, brandishing a voice
and face and hands, poeming: *Naw sugar, I just want to be loved.*
Somewhere a farmer touches himself sober in the stalks.
Somewhere a buzz of feathers and flies ensures nothing goes to waste.
Somewhere, there you are, biting into barbecue sauce draped on a rib.
You tell me you know he loved you. Listened. Gave everything he's got.

———

Brenda,
Sometimes you rattle into my mind and I want to pull the car over
and mold myself an ax. They say we're dust, right? We can cry ourselves
into mud, reshape our bodies, harden at noon. I was born a missing jewel,
natural as the swamp.

———

She was my favorite nurse. 1984. She wasn't scared by my body.
She didn't twist her mouth, proclaim my beauty through one eye.
When she spoke, her voice buzzing, I sunk into the bayou.
My blood cooled. My lips molten leather.

———

When she left:

A beaten girl curls up under him, croons of a sweet Jesus.
Exhaled smoke unveils the exit lights.
The field misses her hands.
The scarecrows tell me they hang themselves.

——

I found a letter in the bayou, in the remains of a molded ax.
It was all in Arabic, the same as my name.
At the end, a voice:
find me.

When the Song Is Done

For a moment, the song is killing you.
Because it is perfect. This song
was made for your sorrow, this *specific* sorrow
from this most exact and exquisite backhand of your life.

The music is ugly, in the way a lover is once they've turned
their back to you, when you know the silence after is all yours,

inelegant, inarticulate, merciless. But dear god, when the music plays,
when it plays, for every moment you'd spent swallowing the burst,
the music is a middle and ring finger at the back of your throat.
And now, for the three minutes and forty-four seconds of this song,
when it retches out of you, it is exactly right. Every chord
is an extracted image of you, convulsing in the shower,
frozen under moon, pounding your mattress,
heaving in the car. These moments are knitted together,
Frankensteined by the sound.

And now,
for a moment, the song
is over. And it is now that you know,

after all the therapy, the pills, the fucking and the sleep,
you know how long the *repeat* button has kept you alive.

How To Make It Gospel

On the television a capella competition The Sing Off, a sextet named Jerry Lawson and The Talk of the Town sung a version of House of the Rising Sun. Afterwards one of the judges asked, How did you make that song a gospel?

The lesson:
open the song with a river of *ooo's*,
thick and low, as if sung under the breath,
spine bent in the field,

a sleeping infant on your back,
the impending moon the only white
you can stand.

You follow with stacking of *doo's*,
surprising the listeners, drawing the
left corner of their mouths into half a smile.

The key to the spell
is not to drag them into the dark,
but to *draw* them in;

when they've had enough
they can always
run out on their own.

Next, you replace the *doo's* with lyrics,
with words, with voices
speaking, layers of them.

And then, the words vanish,
lyric giving way to the *aahh's,*
the *aahh's*, the sounds of holler and howl,

from throats that have ceased to restrain,
the holler and howl have sung for so long,
so God-forgiving long, that it has literally

found its own music, has evolved in key,
has grown out of its soil of agony,
is now some rusted species of joy.

And it is now, once the voices
have done their work,
everyone on the stage

forgets that this is any kind
of god-damned stage, forsakes
the conceit of cameras and lights;

every man in that song is wrapped
in a coil of ghosts,
and the room has surrendered

with them; no one knows what year it is.
No one knows what side of the house
they should be sitting in,

no one will remember who is
supposed to be running, or why the six black men
on the stage have not been dragged away,

nor why they would have followed the men
and their summoning voices,
followed them anywhere.

At last, you summon the hush.
The hush: here, light
as knees on splinters

in the shack. The hush: warm
as the air in the field, as the child on your back,
as muscles of arms raised at the noon.

And the listeners, stunned in their chairs,
will almost forget to clap, for the chair next to them
is no longer someone they knew,

but someone so old, so dark,
they are caught between
apology and humming, as if

sins simply wait for the right song
to burn to, as if they were only born
to be ashed away.

Don't Bother Writing It Down

Every memory is a note. B-sharp. D-flat. G.
Free will is playing our own scales.

My grandma is seventy-eight. As of now
her scale has not shifted. But if it does,

she will forgive me for not listening,
when my face betrays disappointment

that she recounts the succession of notes
in a different order than I believe they were played.

Is this not jazz?, she'll say. *Is this not remix?*
Who am I to tell her what has been diminished.

Blue/Grass

I am victim to banjo and fiddle
turn that voice down
stomps
claps
uproot
my feet crying 1923
these strings know me, take needle, unsew
I'm face down in God's country
I'm swinging
playground of trunks and stumps,
sweaty body in overalls,
legs worn down by the day
I am victim to banjo and fiddle in hands
with green stains for elbows
nails smelling of barnyard and miscarriage
I am midnight runaways, alligator swamps
gospel harmony, savior water dirty
welts on pregnant belly dear god
I am a church shack with a choir of slaves
take the sun back 'til I put my shirt on
I'm tied up in Loretta's clothesline
I am victim of blues and bluegrass
jailbird boots
obsession
I'm gap toothed floorboards shouting wild haired woman
I'm wail of bended note, mercy in A-flat
bleeding fingers for a tireless crowd
I'm birds for shotguns, dirt for tires
old-time delusion, scarecrow's cross
victim of banjo and fiddle
they are burning the house down

ABANDONED HOUSE
for Detroit

When you exist as an abandoned house,
your job is to remain still.
Like the cemetery on the block adjacent to you,
all stirring of souls occurs inside, only.

When a home sheds its dignity in the process
of abandoning, in full view of passersby on Joy Rd,
your last embarrassing moment

of faith is when you think, *at least they'll have the decency
to board me up. Surely they will bury me with my dress on.*

Eviction is a quieting thing,
when, fully awake, you witness the exodus of your organs.
You ignore their request for graceful surrender.
They ignore your request to leave the kettle boiling.

When you've become an abandoned house,
your job is to remain still, to apostle your pride, to
deny the mother's voice in your bedroom ceiling,
deny the father's peppered steak in the kitchen,
deny the son's fantasies in your shower,
to shed the crosses from your walls
as if you yourself never believed.

You try to swallow the music.

You ask Motown to bless someone else's ears;
it is no longer your Saturday, your housecleaning Sabbath,
when broom ushers and choir soap and sweating mops and
scrubbing sermons would wash away your failings
so you could get through another week.

This cleansing is no longer yours. Neither are the diary pages
you shared with every one of them,

when the son left fist marks in your walls to match his father's,
when you formed secret pacts with their smells to reside only here,
when you enveloped bedtime prayers like a midnight mass.

And this is what you will do.

When you accept your calling as an abandoned house,
the cemetery will speak to you. It will tell you that
All Hallow's Eve is a myth, that the dead visit far more than
once a year. It will tell you that when the moon is gone,
and the streets are asleep, they *rise, dance,* shout,
they plug in ether speakers
for block parties
and tear the sky down.

You will listen, and your belly will tell you
when the sky is black,
when the moon is gone,

your closets will open and your dead will rise,
Motown flowing as blood,
father and mother voices scraping the ceilings,
fantasies swirling tornado in the shower,

stove crackling oil and steak, angel hair unbraided,
counters slick and crumbling bread,
kettle singing:

Praising every pulsing God for your cleansing Sabbath,
blessing dusted attic,
your basement and all its bats,

all of you unburied, in mother's dress.
Sky hurtling down. Her midnight mass.

How To Say Goodbye

THERE are times when love slaps you so bad you look at John
Henry and tell him he went out right THE times you want to mold
your devotion into a pair of forty pound hammers and make a hollow
out of the rock DRIVING your way through that mountain muscles
blazing the SOUND of that machine on the other side SPURS you
forward 'cause *ain't no way in hell somethin' else gonna love her as good as
me* YOU look at John Henry bust out the other side only TO sink
to his knees and watch his own guts fall out You MARVEL how his
body gave up
everything

INTERVIEW

Q: *What are the challenges of doing Late Night?*
[The Roots bassist] Owen Biddle: Knowing that the music is at the mercy of whatever else is happening. There will be quick starts and stops on awkward beats, and you have to stay alert and adjust. We had five test shows while the final week of Conan O'Brien's show was filming across the hall, and their band would look in and give us advice and encouragement. [Conan O'Brien bassist] Mike Merritt reminded me about the camera aspect; he said, "Never close your eyes on TV!"

They ain't ready to witness the closing eyes
Stage rule: if you can see them, they can see you
Ain't no music to be found in the gut
No one dances with a sleepwalker

Stage rule: if you can see them, *they* can be sleepwalkers
Comic musicians laugh from glass eyes
No one dances for the dream of you
Gift them a night to grin from the gut

Comic musicians laugh: glass > gut
The fourth wall is padded for the sleepwalker
Gift them a night of grins from the eyes
Conan is late night manna, rain smelling of you

The fourth wall is padded from the funk of you
What is the bass line if not apology for the gut
Conan is late night manna, rain for the sleepwalker
Drum roll for the lidded eyes

What is the bass if not eyes for the sleepwalker
Ain't no music you won't finger from the gut
Drum roll, sleepwalker; lid-less gaze of you
They ain't ready for the gut, to witness the closing eyes

Photos of L.A., April 30ᵗʰ, 1992

1
Buy a new video camera.
Look outside at the flashing lights.
Turn the camera on. Watch
a flock of uniformed flesh pound
him. Know none of their names.
Ignore the turned stomach below
your hands. They are teaching you:
this is how to make a grown man shine.
2
When someone I know mentions that
they have been summoned for jury duty,
neither of us acknowledge the fear.
What power dost such an everyman wield?
Whose decision will it be that burns my city down.
3
When a tear runs down a black man's face,
the words that broke him are normally
I am leaving. I never loved you. Mama's dead.
But today? *Not guilty.*
Maybe he knew what was coming.
He was a pastor. The Lord may have whispered
straight into his right eye: *lock your doors, son.*
Tomorrow, it will pain you to be black.
4
Florence and Normandie: the intersection
that became a roil of fire.
5
A young man, standing next to a blaze,
holds a sign that says *We Will Not Rest.*
Neither of us knows whether the flames
or the sign were less necessary.

6
Here, son. Carry this out. Cops'll be here soon.
Why we stealing, dad?
The city done bad, son. They hurt a black man.
Ain't we black, dad?
7
A definition of failure:

a group of looters
forced to lie face down
under the watch of the police

on Martin Luther King Jr. Blvd.
8
If the world were indeed flat,
perhaps riots would present lesser
consequence, would have no ability
to reach around the planet to scar the
left shoulder of the one that just hurled
a bottle at some stranger's car.
9
There must be an equation for this,
some mathematical theorem for what makes
a wayward black man's beating into a pulsing
national anthem into a writhing city of bottles
into a Korean shop owner guarding his store
with a handgun. How does a black shop owner
with the words "Black Owned" spray painted on his
store have to wear a bulletproof vest? How
does *We love you Rodney* shard our own glass?

IMMOLATION

The shooting stopped at once. The street was still,
save for the screams from a witness here or there,
and the guns all found themselves lying on the ground.
It was Pookie, the stutterer, who after all their years
of jokes had finally found something to say. For this moment,
there were no Crips or Bloods, just black people watching
a black person set himself on fire, silent, shaking,
as if an East Side saint, borne from the light.

CHARLES RILEY

You go by Lil Buck but
your name is Charles Riley, as if
rocking a hip hop name to conceal
the ballet in your pop locking
body. On your toes, you spin
on your ankles, you bend, gleefully stealing
the plié in your bones slipping home
unscathed, the languishing piano
subsumed in your Memphis grit
as if the entire black renaissance
were reborn here, in the flesh
of a young black man at risk
of being swallowed down
of absorbing an older music
in the haunt of falling

You don't belong here
dancing in the baroque man's attic
Nina, Eunice Waymon, harbinger of
holyfied rage, surging from your
hands loaded, always at the ready
the zip gun wrapped in chords
glowering from the hate in your mouth
dreaming of burying Debussy in black
its hunger for penance swallowing it whole
dancing on the tongue until forgiveness
of a burning bloomed into a grace
with no fear of closing one's eyes
knowing the slow cooked and salted joy
born in your hands
sweat suckled from the ground

SAUDADE
(THERE ARE NO FOULS IN STREETBALL)

When shooting
baskets,
alone,
at night,
in that light rain,
the rules change.
Your hands find the ball before your eyes will.
You aren't built for the nocturne.
Your tongue is not the snake's; it leads you nowhere.

The streetlights only help from a distance,
as when the slithering orange pierces your glasses,
it bends into unwanted stars.

The ball is wet. There is beauty in an acknowledged
lack of grip. Form over friction:
grief is a team game you practice alone.

When you insist on shooting a three,
you will not see the ball's fate,
but you can hear the clank. Hear
the swish.

And the feet.
There is no wandering here.
To a watcher's flashlight-ed eye,
you may appear to stumble, stutter.
This is rain choreography.
Night toes en pointe.

And then the game.
You invent the stiff-backs,
the drag-footers, shit-talkers,
the slick and quiet foul-ers.
You take no free throws. You dance 'em down.

You don't "settle" for the jump shot. You kill with it.
This, at least, you have earned.

At some point, you look up, as if her ghost
has nothing to do in the ether but watch.

You remember shooting on this court earlier,
in the baby dusk, you at one hoop,
another dude at the other,
til he leaves after announcing, *I don't do lightning.*
You stay after this, wondering how a lick
of electric could feel to an already fried body.

Three years after her death,
I can swish a triple with my left hand.
This comes from practice,
from sublimating fury,
from a music
that on this night

floods the body,
through a reverb of rain.

Hip-Hop Yoga

1
Your throat chakra is cracked open by the snare.
Your head rocks with the stress of the neck.
The beat booming in your chest, you bloom into a sixteen bar Boddhisattva.

2
You hear a hissing nearby, as if from a snake, but you know now
it is spray paint. Your north side temple is being tagged.

3
Your body stretches forward, bent back, straight spine,
hands posed behind you, locked at the wrist.
You whisper *namaste* while bent over a cop car.
The uniformed man behind you speaks but you hear no human in his voice.

4
Eyes closed, you meditate to the music
bouncing from the speakers in your car.
It is the longest red light on MLK Boulevard.

5
You bought this suit because it was both professional
and flexible. Every job interview is a downward facing dog.
You update your resume in a handstand.
You are a praying mantis at the bus stop.

6
They call it Savasana, the Corpse Pose.
Your nephew has learned it so well, is so relaxed,
through your tears you wonder if he is still
breathing from the hole in his chest.

7
Meditation: You've no words to describe the DJ
materializing from the dust, levitating cross-legged
four feet in the air. His hands are poised above a record and needle.
The record spins a glorious Nothing.

8
Before the beatbox there was the mouth.
Before the microphone there was the throat.
Before the spray, before the wall, there were the fingertips and palms
and the lover's body that allowed them.
We were already born weeping to the beat.
We already knew to wave our hands in the air.

9
The breaker is sweating in Pranayama.
The breaker is the vindicating saint. He spins and flips hosannas
on the north side's behalf. His entire choreography is 47 poses
    chained together,
enough to bless every soul at the party. He moves as if we're dying,
as if paradise has an expiration date. His hands balance and propel,
feet sliding and spinning, his torso the burnt flesh singing in tongues.

10
One forgiveness later, you are home with a bouquet of groceries in
    your arms.
Your husband slowly washes your feet.
Together, you speak nothing of nirvana. Nothing to break the hush
of loving the food away.

GEORGE GERSHWIN WRITES JANIS JOPLIN UPON HEARING HER VERSION OF *SUMMERTIME*

Until the doctors confirmed my tumor,
everyone believed I was faking it.
I attempted to push my chauffeur out of a moving car.
I could convince no one of the oppressive scent of burning trash.
Once, while performing, I forgot my music. Hands poised in the air.

On the way out of a restaurant,
the air was rubber and flame. I collapsed.
Someone ordered me to stand.

I tell you this to say, aside from the tumor,
I was not terribly unhappy.
Just enough.

I wrote *Summertime* for *Porgy and Bess*, in Charleston, South Carolina,
working in the fields with the Gullahs, dancing with them,
soaking in the spirituals until I could conjure them myself.
I worked long enough to know I couldn't call it a theft.

I was overcome with the rhythms. The steps and claps
accompanying the voices, wail and thigh slap,
this was not my home. But we did love.

I wrote *Summertime* unaware I was dying.

And this is what I want to tell you.
Rhapsody in Blue was written on a train
to the rhythm of the tracks.
The staccato of taxi cars informed *An American In Paris*.

The haggard breath, ribbed violin, is most chilling in whisper.
And when you walk out of a restaurant only to bow to the ground,
the collision is a bassoon weeping itself dry.

Did you hear, when those Gullah voices
cast a net over the dark?
That was the morning I awoke to sand crabs
invading my room. It was not the sickness;
I did not imagine this.

It was the rhythm of a soil that cannot forget,
of hands tapping a tired flesh;
a throat's humid memory of anything but ease.

ONE IN A MILLION

To Aaliyah's brother who, after the plane crash that killed her, was asked to
re-dub some of her lines in her final film

When it was done, when the film editing could resume,
when they thanked you and flew you home,
I wonder how long it took before you could speak
aloud. Rashad, how did you not lose your mind?
When my friend passed away, her mother told me she
once called her number, a year later,
and hung up, so that when the new owner called
back, her phone would again buzz with her daughter's name.
How did you not wake up one morning
with twenty voice mails on your cell,
after using every pay phone in the city to call yourself
by name? When your parents called, did they ever hesitate
to hang up? Does your throat still constrict
when you whisper *goodnight*?

Slow

The bullet, itself, is swift.
Once released, it wastes no time
arriving where it belongs.
This, in itself, is not special.

When a hunted activist is finally
murdered, the stopping heart
is but the epilogue;
the original sacrifice began

with the shedding of all doubt
that their godly work was also
a promise to die, with no one
to know when, or how:

after Malcolm's office is shot,
after his house is bombed,
after the poison in his dinner
is subverted only by a physician
and a pump, the imagination, once

a beauty in itself, begins to hound
you. The contract your life has signed
demands that every mundanity smell like
death: breakfast is never again

eaten without prayer. Driving
to the store cannot occur without
a key and ignition, and when the
engine turns a second too slowly

you wait... as if a suicide bomber waiting
for God to set you off.
Seventy times a day, every following

day you have not yet died, the waiting
must have felt like a volcano

of laughing, churning in the belly.
You are terrified

of the moment your wife whispers
goodnight. You attend your daughter's
school play with your own gun
in your jacket. The cashier at the grocery store

is staring, waiting for you to remove
your hand from your pocket.

And the next night, when the
killing at last arrives, when the bullet has
sung its chord of *hello-forgive-goodbye,*
is the falling ever a relief?
Are the screams blooming around you

a delayed eruption, as if your own
rolling eyes were silently laughing?

Isis

"Arm. Hand. Foot. Calf. Thigh.
These: the five ways to love him."
—*Anonymous*

After more than a year, after her husband's
body was cut into thirteen pieces, scattered throughout
the Midwest, she has nearly all of him.

Once,
after discovering the second hand, in a sewer in Indiana,
after hissing at the rats nipping at it, after her breath lit them
into ash, she returned home. To a freezer of two hands,
an arm and a thigh. This once did she indulge herself,
just enough, weeping slightly into the spoilt meat,
joining the right hand and arm at the wrist.
This once, she whispered a trio of ancient words,
then watched the hand slowly open,
close. She then took a paring knife and separated them.
She knew, if careless, there was still time for her to go mad.

Now, with the torso gingerly retrieved from
a junkyard in Detroit, the scent of the rust
even stronger than the death, the torso lying
on the backroom floor, she can finally

link the arms to hands;
link the thigh, to calf,
to foot, thigh to calf to
foot.

Her husband is once again taller than her.
Long enough to leave the freezer for their bed.

She carries him there, lies them down,
buries her screams. She has nearly all of him.
Just enough, to lie down.
Just enough, to wrap around.

Soon, she will recover
the head, the pelvis. Then the work will be done:

it is then that she will mouth the final words,
watch the breath invade his lungs, then retreat
in a coughing fit. It is then that his eyes will slowly rebirth
his gaze, when their locking eyes will know the magic
can only sustain the reunion for an hour,
that there is no time for anything but lovemaking,
as mad as two can ever be in the face of the clock:

it is then that she will receive him for the last time
in this house. She will feel the life jetting through her,
into her, the quiet conception. She will feel the stirring
of her son before her husband is, once again,
still.
She will sleep for an hour, then dress
and catch the 21 to work.

The beauty of living in the city
is that no one believes she's a goddess.
No one would question why she'd
stalk the strewn pieces of the love of her life.
The beauty of living in the city

is that no one will see you
holding hands with a hand;

no one will ask
why it is holding you back.

To the Cats
for ten-year-old Ashlynn Conner

To the cats she never met:

if you were human, in your poverty
you would find a reason to curse
the universe, asking why it never
protected you enough. But the truth
is that though you are ill, though you are tired,
there were two healing hands preparing for you.
A budding veterinarian, lover of the homeless cat,
she just didn't have the time. Not with a heart
too easily pierced by the words of the other kids,
so easily run into the ground. Not with a mind
that had seen enough television to know
that once she'd had enough, there was a way out.

To the cats she loved:

please, stop visiting her porch.
There is a reason her scent has grown fainter.
When her mother sees you
her shoulders begin to shake.
There is a reason that when
you visit her porch, staring at the front door,
there is a sound from inside that you remember,
the sound at night when the alley cats mourn for the kitten run down
by the speeding car. The cacophony of mewling,
accusing the moon, shredding the spine.

But know: when she was here, you felt her hands at their best,
stroking the underbelly of a world that had no interest
in clawing her down.

How To Say Goodbye

There is a reason Johnny Cash could *cover* a song so deeply that it no longer belonged to Nine Inch Nails He was seven months from *death*, singing this song *as if* he had written it for his wife as if these were the lyrics he had been *hunting* down for 30 years There is a delicacy to the art of apology to eviscerating yourself in honor of the one whose *devotion* you'd wasted I can only imagine what June felt as she heard it the very first time how many years of trembling knuckles had *returned to* her fragile hands *Wonder* how many times she tried to tell him there's nothing to forgive

On Meeting My Mother's Father for the First Time

I first met my grandfather in 1955.
He did not know me. I was hidden in a woman's face,
21 years old, pregnant from a love he'd promised was hers alone.
I loved his twinkling gaze and railroad hands, so good at holding her
    in place.

His voice blurs, a spatter of shadows, drowned out
by the cries exiting this woman's mouth,
as she learns the truth of this man,
of the wife that he'd already had. Leaving town, soundless,
to Chicago,

she believed the myth of distance making a man smaller,
promising that she'd never come back.

The second time I met my grandfather, fifty years later,
he did not know my voice. It was wrapped in a woman's,
his daughter's, as she finally decided to track him down, and call.

I remember his voice, coarse velvet, slinking through
the phone, offering something tangible; basement and flooring
for a bottomless house. This was not the man who'd uprooted

my grandmother's heart. This was something else, a spectre
I didn't know how to bury. Here he was, humming
benevolent bass into my mother's open ear. He was real.
The storybook flooded unto itself.

The third time I met my grandfather, he did not know me.
I did not let him. In this moment, in a humble church in Cleveland,
my mother smiled as I shook his cavernous hand.
My father grinned, my brother was quiet.
My grandmother did not come.

I watched my mother hand him a photo album. He sat next to me.
I stiffened.

I split.
I was my mother, sharing the life he'd never known she had.
I was my grandmother, silent.
I am myself, shuddering at the intimacy he's been allowed to see:

me as an infant, naked in a sink;
my parents, kissing and young;
my brother and I in graduation gowns;
my grandmother with hair done, filling a summer dress,
wearing her oldest skin.

Her heart simmers in my jaw; it will not move.
He tells me he would like to know me.
I cannot tell him how he already had.

It is August, 1956. Chicago.
I am holding the infant daughter
that man may never meet.
She is everything I'd believed in him,
everything he'd desired in me.
She will not carry his name.

She will wear the faintest shape
of his face. Her voice
all air and attic.
All the rest is precious.
All of her, mine.

CRIBBAGE, OR CRIB, BITCH

So this one time I was playing cards with my mother
and a few of her friends. I was a kid, and barely understood
the rules to this game, but that didn't stop the shit talk from
flying freely and often, and hard. At one point I got so angry
that I told my mother, from the other end of the table, that
if she wasn't my mother I would hit her in the face.
The table froze, a lone syllable of shit talk poking its head
from one friend's dropped jaw. I imagine the friends were wondering
if my mother would murder me now. Wondering if it would be their
job to hold me down while she retrieved the knife, as if
they were all bound by some silent code, something about unity
when abuse rears its adolescent head. Wondering if
my mother would show mercy, choosing peace, only for them
to finish the job instead, as if quietly vowing, *it won't be my daughter
this fool goes to jail lovin'. Not now, boy. Never again.*

LOST

As of yesterday, her ex-husband is dead. She is seventy.
I am twenty-nine, with no idea how I'll get there.
But I know there was a time I wanted to be seventy, with you.

I imagine, if it happened, if you were the one to die first,
when the news hit, I'd ask, *what time?*
When they told me 7:29pm, I'd strain to remember

what I was doing, at that moment, on that day. The terror
is that I'll remember that I was not pre-occupied
with something vibrant or vital;

I had just felt nothing.

I am not ready for seventy. To endure this last, patient bite
for walking away.

The space between hands and the skin that no longer wants them
The space between a body split into two houses and lives
The space between lungs born to expel each other
The space between the final cruelties that broke our lust in half
The space from the hand to the phone
The space that nightly lights into a howl

The moment
when your flickering, dying mind strains to frame
a blurred shot of me, when something dimming inside
you says, *Lost One. For this, you were supposed to be here.*

RIFLE

Some of my friends are alarmed when they discover my love
for playing Buck Hunter. My fixation.
Not wanting to waste a shot.

I really jazz for the stance,
plastic butt pressed into shoulder,
the stillness before the first virtual bullet.

I learned that stance as a small thing, in Raleigh, North Carolina.

Grandma's brother, bearer of my middle name, my favorite summer visit,
my only tangible reason when aching for the South.
I'd never felt blacker, riding that bike down proud dirt roads
tan as my palms, the dust rising in clouds 'til I had to stop.
The inexplicable need to stay on guard.

I loved when he took us out back,
when he handed me a rifle with his critter-killing hands.

The kick-back taught me to fear it.
I learned to set my feet, own its weight, thicken my eardrums
'til I had some bass for my snare.

Those soda cans, fifty feet away, were pressure points of initiation.
He told me I was small,
but not too small.

When our lesson ended, I hated the ache that came.
I knew how good I could be, if I stayed here in Raleigh,
Uncle William's cool voice guiding my hands,

but I was a city boy. Didn't belong here.
Had to settle for a one-night stand with the heat.
Had to try to remember the smell of a blacker sweat,
                              the rifle's thunder crack.

I don't even know when he died.
He's just my middle name now.
But there's a fierceness to my finger. Feet set.

I ain't so small, Raleigh. You ain't so heavy now.

Apology To a House Party

"I suddenly realized what it was to be Black in America in 1963, but it wasn't an intellectual connection of the type Lorraine had been repeating to me over and over—it came as a rush of fury, hatred and determination. In church language, the Truth entered into me and I `came through.' "
—Nina Simone

It ain't their fault. They just like good music.
But Nina Simone was never built for a house party.

There is too much dissonance, too many swapping of masks
when we casually stroll into someone else's house. This living

room is presumably where something *lives*,
heated and blood pumped, where two nights before

this room could have hosted the knockdown, drag-out
shouting match of their lives. Well-placed pictures

can be more than decoration. There could be a wasted
orgasm lying in the dishwasher. But damn if we

won't polish up our nice, offer it
as bandage for the sawed off thigh.

Damn if it just got a little awkward, if in the dusk of
a punch line someone wept for a miscarriage.

In this house, pleasantry was born in a manger.
In this house, swallow your divorce and praise the meatballs.

And damn if, in a haze of murmur and wine, Nina Simone doesn't slip
into the room, if the stereo doesn't sound like it's melting

as her voice trickles upon your tongue from a third world faucet.
Nina is *here*. We barely deign to notice. And this is where I have failed.

Nina whispers me something damaged, reminds me
I'm the only black person in the room,

marveling how the curtains are reduced to ash;
the finger foods smell like they were torn from the vine.

This was one of those songs that I'd taken home
and soaked in, when a dormant grief awakens in your blood

and you live it all over again, but now it is glistening, feverish,
wanting, like black folks singing opera. This house party

is the Metropolitan, is Donald Trump singing *Porgy and Bess*,
and damn if I can't say this aloud, can't

turn up the stereo without permission, announce to the startled room:
For the next three minutes we need to shut the fuck up.

Nina Simone's giving birth while we stare at the wall.
She is hunched over the coffee table wailing *Mississippi Goddam*,

she's pounding the floor, staining the carpet.
And if I were a braver man, I'd be raving right with her:

the room would freeze as I stared at them like 1963,
cried out to no one *Medgar is dead*, telling them how one night,

after the bombing of four little girls, she had had enough
of playing the Passive Black, tried to build a homemade zip gun to cut

down some white people but stopped
herself and sat at her piano.

In this house of sweaters and laughter,
my silence is a drowning.

If I were a braver man, this room could have been quieted
enough to be gifted with a shivering,

from everything we thought we'd left at the door,
in the car, in the ashtray, the dryer,

in the silence of a stereo that has completed a summoning,
the trembling hand's vibrato, the emptied glass.

From Leadbelly To Kurt Cobain

My girl, my girl, don't lie to me
Tell me where did you sleep last night?
In the pines, in the pines, where the sun don't never shine
I shivered the whole night through

You do understand, son, what happens.
When the song is done?
You *do* know that woman is dead.

See, the way I hear that song, when you
covered it on that TV show, in front
of all them innocent lil' vanilla chirren,
it sounded like you thought that woman
was still there. That was funny.
Singin' like you was havin' a quarrel
before cuddlin' under a blanket.
You tickled me, son.
'Cause fact is that quarrel
had already come. And gone.

Now what I *did* like was you got
the passion, full strum, you take your time,
like that song was the love of your life
and after a late night she called you poison
and now in that bed every thrust of your body
feels like shortenin' her life. Yeah, son. I hear you.

But there's a reason they call it the blues.
They ain't singin' the reds. Not a lick of fuchsia
to be found. It's the blues 'cause it's quiet.

You's a good boy. Ain't never killed nobody.
Once you done it, it stays with you.
Will Stafford stays with you.
The woman you killed him over is gone.
(That there's the bitch.)
And if you talk about it, you don't never get loud.

'Course, there's more practical reasonin' at work too, see,
I made my money playin' my cuddly lil' songs for
smoother faces than you, folks that couldn't imagine the killin'
grounds they drove over on the way to my show.
I sing like I wanna,
I wouldn't make my money.

If I had me a shoutin' license like you,
if I coulda hollered and tramped my way 'round
the stage like Jesus himself was filled
with the devil and asked me to stomp it out,
if I sang so hard Will Stafford rose from the dirt
and cursed me for killin' him 'til I shot him again,

if I coulda bled this song like that,
I'da dragged my dead woman's body
on the stage and sang it to her face.

It'd be perfect, son. If I coulda sang it
like that, the silent room filled with the scent of her dress,
oh, son. I wouldn't have to explain a thing.

Revenant

The body does not know what world
it lives in. This is why when I dream of falling
from a cliff, my body shocks awake,
heart blasting a scream it no longer needs.
Where the soul moves, the blood will follow.

When your dream returned, on my way out
of my office, at work, just before my hand reached
the door, my tired body remembered you:
Lying on our sides, in someone's bed,
you had lain your cheek in my left hand.

When your dream returned to me
in my office, at work, my heart rioted
in reflex, my veins swelling
from the breath that rose in.
I was angry for only then waking up.

My body rooted itself through the carpet,
felt me leaving, preparing itself to fall.

My left hand is the soil you left so quietly
open. My left hand still believes it is there,
in some room where you are alive,
this left-brain blasphemy.

My left hand does not age. It has not surrendered
a cell of dead skin. It does not waste its grip
calling the soul back.

THE DOOR

—*Interviewer: So you literally mean, as a Witness, you actually knock on
strangers' doors? In Chanhassen? You?*
—*P. Rogers Nelson: Yes.*

And this is your face when you can't mask the shock.
The television's chattering a whiter noise,
the opened door in your right hand suddenly a pillar

as you behold Prince, wrapped in humbling thread,
politely asking if he can speak with you about paradise,
his hair short and dry, his voice

a balm. Your wife's bewildered inquiry from the
living room bends into a gasp as he accompanies
you to your dining room table. The television is black.

As he fingers his book, more smoothly than any microphone
stand, as you nod your head more reflexively than
a waving lighter, your wife's hand upon yours

is the only force holding you to the ground. His gaze
does not waver as you reply that you've never really
devoted a breath to God. On and on he speaks,

as if drawing guidance from your own closet.
You are amazed with your resolve, as thirty minutes
have vanished without you asking, politely:

Shouldn't you be fucking us right now?
His smile implies you would not be the first,
and the Jehovah in his mouth gently fastens you.

But this time, God feels more than a passing,
lower to the tongue, His wafting presence
now a thick baritone coil, as your throat swells to bear

the weight, the grip slipping down past the neck,
the torso suddenly starved. This is the God that
had drunkenly willed the mud into your body,

drinking the cries from your guileless mouth.
When he has vanished, your table is a breaking bed.
Your wife, a witness. His hips, gone.

Anais Washington Carver

"Why, then, should we who believe in Christ be surprised at what God can do with a willing man in a laboratory?" —George Washington Carver

1

At home, in every room in the house, when I walk in, Anais Nin is sitting in the corner. She is writing. That is, when she isn't staring at me. When her insistent gaze seems to ask why I've not opened a diary. In the kitchen, she's next to the sink, in the corner, writing. In the basement, she yawns. She silently accuses me of having a secret. These are the ways I talk with the dead.

The touch of another human does strange things to my skin. Beauty is strange. My skin knows too many languages, forgets who is speaking, right now. Jeff Buckley is singing from somewhere behind me. His voice is strange, in the way it seems to love me. I am shaking a stranger's hand, and Jeff is singing. I am sparring in the gym. Jeff is singing. I am lying naked with a lover that believes she has learned me enough. My skin is babbling to itself, hearing Portuguese but mumbling Spanish. Jeff is singing Italian behind me. I understand it all.

2

Only recently did I learn the truth of George Washington Carver. He was more than the Jesus of peanuts. He was a scientist that credited everything to God. Every morning at 4 a.m., he'd wake and walk in the woods, listening to his god in an unhurried forest. It was there that he asked his god how to undress the veils of the earth, how to coax the ground into keeping his world alive. He was ridiculed for his lack of measurable methods, for trusting so deeply in the unproven, unseen. He was a man unafraid of living in two worlds at once.

3

From some world I have not seen, a young boy has arrived at my door. His eyes tell me he is my son. If I let him survive. If I can love the world in front of me as deeply as that which we cannot see. I tell him that everything I believe is maddeningly unseen. He is unseen. Jeff is unseen. Carver is unseen. I am an artist, and this is my only saving grace.

I'm writing about a child only I have seen, holding him to me as if there were no difference between the unborn and the dead.

4

I am lying in a hospital bed. On my right is a surgeon. On my left is a holy man. With every incision the surgeon makes, the holy man is unearthing the memory I had stored there, in that rib, that vein. The surgeon does not know I am awake, remembering every cell of the cancer he is trying to remove, remembering every reason someone on this earth gave me a reason to dissolve.

5

I am in the forest, at some ungodly hour. No one else is here. Lying in the dirt, my skin swears something is speaking. Coaxing it into breathing. As if our bodies could also be prayed to, could be slowly coaxed into staying alive.

JOHN THE BAPTIST

If the Second Coming were to manifest, it would be preceded,
again, by John the Baptist,

his voice primed for a new wilderness,
dressed in vintage rags and untamed hair,

his bare feet dragging along the dusted cement, communing invisibly
with monks and friars, plumbers and bus drivers,

dancing tightrope on rain-slick telephone wires.
His eyes would narrow on Sundays, his presence only apparent
when, on cue, every infant in the congregation starts crying.

The graveyards would reciprocate greeting; even the larvae would freeze.
His cheeks would stream at the edge of a river that was once his,
dipping his feet in mortal memory.

The holy land's heat would hum in him, as it always had,
the sweat trickling between his toes whispering: *Jerusalem,
Israel, lover, Essene*. In the city,

he'd moan empathetic for every soul taught to despise the flesh,
shuddering in their memories of the mirror, their rudderless guilt,
rumble Ave Maria for crumpled fathers in the shower.

He'd save his softest prayers for that mental hospital,
down in Nowhere, Georgia,
the one he'd finally hunted down.

His eyes would burn holes in their straitjackets,
fingers twitching in hunger for the devil.
Under their breaths, he would hum the middle name of Salome,

finger the memory of his neck, blink back the splitting and platter.
Her ageless scent would lead him through the labyrinth of halls,
his borrowed flesh blurring through the door of her room,

the girl he'd been looking for, the youngest descendant,
mumbling into her knees the scrapped windshields
of a perfect Aramaic.
He'd watch her try to remember how to dance.

Finally, his lips would warm her forehead, bless her still.
Precious, he'd say, *our work is finished*.

Tudor Remedies in the Age of Obama

Asthma
Swallow young frogs or live spiders coated in butter.

Some would prefer that fear boast a measurable,
physical consequence. May they offer their miracle
tanks when we can hardly bear to breathe.

Whooping Cough
Find a ferret, feed it with milk, then give the leftover milk to sick child.

I work in a school where extra paper clips are cigarettes for lifers.
Few of our children can read an analog clock.

Bubonic Plague
Hold a live chicken against the sores until the bird dies.

We're a long way from Tuskegee and syphilis.
Now they just play with our houses.

Rheumatism
Wear the skin of a donkey.

Taylor Swift should
thank him.

Gout
*Boil a red-haired dog in oil, then add worms and the marrow from pig bones;
apply the mixture.*

Alchemy: Melting a rifle and molding it into a camera phone.
Discipline: Holding the camera phone still as a black boy is stomped.
    While handcuffed.
Breakthrough: Someone finally figures out how to take a cop down.

Headache
Rub the forehead with a rope used to hang a criminal.

Today's breakfast: Country-fried bailout.

Jaundice
Drink a pint of ale containing nine drowned head lice every morning for a week.

Young people "don't vote." Ghetto people "don't vote."
Exactly how many times shall one settle for head
and feel respected in the morning?

Deafness
Mix the gallstone of a hare and the grease of a fox, warm the result, and place it in the ear.

Retrospect: A rapper once said his president didn't care about black people.
The miracle: This remark was recently deemed by said president as
    the lowest blow of his term.
Lower than the hurricane, the towers.
Revelation: The rapper was partly wrong. His president listened.

Warts
*Lay half a mouse on the wart for half an hour and then bury it in the ground.
As the mouse rots, the wart will vanish.*

When the governor of Virginia tried to omit slavery
from Confederate History Month, I could hear

Michelle's drowsy voice: *Barry,
please stop shooting. Photos can't run.*

Hashtags

Moses tags Harriet Tubman on Twitter:

So what you're saying is,
all those complaints, all those years, all those miles,

all I needed was a gun??
#Damn #lol not really #smmfh

THE BORROWED MOUTH

In the 1780s, George Washington was nearly toothless,
and hired a dentist to transplant new teeth into his jaw.
These teeth were (willingly) extracted from the mouths of his slaves.

It is a wonder that his speeches were delivered without incident,
that some soul possession did not occur in the pawnshop of his mouth,

that an audience of men did not return home from an officers' meeting
with ashen face and hastened voice, did not whisper to their wives
how Washington spoke as if gripped by a puppet master,

how his words jumped jagged between *my countrymen* and **lord,**
we convene today and **my baby,** *in the interest of Congress* and
please God bring him back. It is a wonder that his eyes

did not cross themselves in horror, as his jaw snapped open beyond
the limits the Lord designed, that his lower lip did not drip a litany
of blood, that no negro colored hand reached out from his throat,

escaping grave soil after being buried, mid-thrash.

Bachmann's Harlem

And this is the version of history
where, after the Battle of Little Bighorn,
an unharmed George Custer sits at his table,
elevated boots muddying the edge,
sipping the blood of a vanquished Indian
delicately from a wine glass,

> where a victorious tea party blots Chardonnay
> onto every historical record of a redeemed America,
> where children are freed to imagine a nation
> with no fields to forgive,

where graffiti on tenement walls
is but an artifact from an older Harlem,
when zoot suits and tap dancing could
never save a life, when marches were
but vanity's invention for women,

> where Mary Todd Lincoln, in 1875, rests
> warmly in an asylum in Batavia, Illinois,
> thankful for the forcing of sleep, freed
> from the shadow of her felled magnolia,
> her children waiting to kiss her prodigal cheek,
> once she arises to let herself out.

ADA, OR 23 LETTERS THE MUTE WOMAN PLAYS AT THE PIANO
—after the film "The Piano"

1. I did not build this. I waited.

2. When the piano tuner is late, I adjust my ears.
    Higher, lower. I must speak. I will not wait for him.

3. My hands hurt when I have not said enough.

4. There. Lay your hand there. No lower. Yes, right there.

5. There would be no war if we all could prance about naked.
    Daily. How could we harm such bellies? Dare we abuse such humble
    folds?

6. That man is not my husband. I was shipped. He is my keeper.

7. Here. Here. Hold here. Still. Let go.

8. This dress. This fabric, choking. Lover. Hang me. Hang me
    from my dress.

9. My keeper is jealous. He knows. I do not love him.

10. I know when you are listening. When your hips shiver first.

11. One day, the piano will drown. I will attempt to carry it
    on a boat too frail and it will fall. This I have seen in my dream.
    I know you are building a boat.

12. Bury me when I am gone. But not in a box.

Lay me directly in the dirt. Let it slowly digest and grow me again.

13. My keeper cried last night when, again, I would not touch him.
    He bruised my waist.

14. My hands hurt.

15. This fabric, choking.

16. He cut off my finger. He—he

17. The bloo—it—list-listen—list—me—can youhearmecan—

19.

21. Tune. No. Tun—

22. Dress. Hold. Choke. Death. Hold. Why—won't we—die—won't we—No.

23. Love. Ad.just.Ear.s. I.still.play.foryou.

HER

The one that stopped the war.
The one that ended it again.
The one who served bread baked in light.
Whose lotion scent entered his dream as a comet.
Who tore the reddened dress.
That got drunk and shaved her head.
Whose belly hissed like a burnt bush.
The one allergic to fruit.

My hallucination:

The one standing in front of me.
Who is four years old.
Whose gaze knows no man taller than me.
Whose voice adores the vowels in *Daddy*.

GLADDAVIA

1

Your child is in your hands. Newborn, and literally small enough to cry in your hands. Holding her, you are frozen; you must choose a name. What will this brown-skinned girl answer to for the remainder of her life? It is a question you've lived with for months, and at first it was funny. As a black person you can name your child anything. You can invent a name based on the vowels you like the best, or spell a more common name with incoherent letters, so that when anyone reads it on paper they will be too rattled to pronounce it correctly. If you're romantic, you can combine the names of the family members you loved the most, so that each syllable is a grave opening, footsteps on the grass. Whatever you choose, it will be permanent, your most indelible imprint on the world. Finally, you have chosen: Gladdavia.

2

Learning a new name is a cavernous magic: Ousmane, Travares, Dezarai, Ramarley, Chianti, Laquanta, Sheketah, Trayvon, Gladdavia. It is the intimacy of mangling a new instrument, the humility of tripping while learning an immigrant dance. It is a challenge we did not ask for upon meeting this person, upon sharing an office with him, upon picking up the paper and reading of his murder, but it is a challenge we accept. We remember.

3

We black folk are known for our children's names. They are designed to be remembered. It's as if somewhere within, we have already seen the day that our son goes to a party, or to a grocery store and fails to come back. It's as if we have already seen the bullet, the knife, the taser, have already known the murder will not have been just, and that all too soon the nation will be crying to the heavens with your child's name: Ousmane, Travares, Trayvon, Ramarley. You must have known that your child's name would need to be remembered, to force its way into a stranger's outraged mouth.

4

Your daughter is missing. She has been missing for four years, and no one but you is still waiting for her. She had the misfortune of being both kidnapped and black. But still, you believe, because one day the phone will be warm in your hand, you will hear a voice you are afraid to recognize, a voice cracked hoarse by beatings in the woods, a voice you will spend years washing from her mouth. And you know when you ask who is calling, when the cracking voice tremors in tune with your own, when you hear the name *Gladdavia*, you will know she is *yours*. You carry her name swaddled in your mouth, replaying every syllable of the call that does not come. You believe. You gave her the name that allows this. Your brown-skinned Gladdavia was born to come back.

K's Diner

We talk about twice a year, and every time,
you remind me that I owe you *that* poem.
I remind you that it ain't happening;
that poem and its writer are gone.
But if it means anything, the poem was good.

It's my fault for waiting too long.
It's not like the love left,
but when I decided to release an impossible
thing, the words went with it.
You're relegated to music. At this point
I could only dance it. But I'm not foolish
enough to serenade you with my body.

If I were to ever leave this country,
I imagine that there would always be an unpaved street
reaching for me, that some nowhere diner
would whisper of a chili cheeseburger
perfectly built to birth my babies.
Even then, I would send it a postcard
from the city that watched my youngest kiss,
then leave.

The difference is that I have not truly left.
I just stop talking to you. And when I fail
to avoid you, when the phone slips into my hand
and your voice trips into my ears, you ask me about
that poem. And I feel a little guilty.
So here's my compromise.

Go half on my plane ticket.
Give me the key to your apartment.
Leave.

When you return, there will be dishes on the floor.
I won't have broken your favorites. And all of them
will be washed. When you open the stove,

there will be a watermelon. With a marker
I'll have nicknamed it Texas.

After you've sliced a piece
and carried it to the couch, you'll notice your TV screen
has been replaced by a mirror. While you gaze
at Mirror You, over your Mirror Shoulder
there will be a shadow. You will ask if it's me.
You will know the intimacy of a death that
stays with you, stretching your lungs,
teasing your sanity. Somehow, every mark on your
walls will spell the word *beloved*. Every time it
will grow louder, biting, until you're bent over the bathtub
hacking it out. You will adore the hacking, and in fact
believe that prior to this moment your throat had never
hollered its god. The shower is spraying,
was that your hand?
your clothing is shredded,
was that your hand?

the soap is fucking with you.
How can a bar of Ivory smell like
every human body you have loved?

Your bed has been waiting. Under the blanket
you swear there is a sleeping child. You mouth her name,
and even that is too loud, our child is crying,
your hands reaching for her as you sink to the floor.
Your instinct tells you she is looking for the night light.
But you are already crawling under the bed.
Just for tonight, this is where we belong:

her cries dripping through the mattress.
Her music filling our head.

We are the monster.
We are the monster.

Rosa Parks (or Blue/Grass, Part II)

50 Cent is playing violin
in Kentucky, summer of 1865.

He's in the middle of a Rebel's revival, floor-stomping,
bearded and hollering, his fingers a spider leg choir.

They're all drunk on his vitamin water, sweaty hands in gang signs;
the room is so dark, none of them notice he's black.

Lil Kim is in labor, ninety-six hours and counting,
her mouth devoid of verses,

her breasts unaware of the presence of gravity.
She is hollering in an abandoned shack.

Mary J. is trying to assist, failing.
The baby is too sexy to come out.

Eminem is standing upright on a speeding horse,
screaming *he doesn't give a fuck* (invisible windows down,

inner system up). He's broken
his last gold record in half,

using the jagged edges to free the gangsta from his wrists,
drive-by spraying a Lil Wayne lynch mob.

50 Cent

doesn't know why he has a violin,
can't explain his devotion and closed eyes,

but the sound carries him upward, eclipsing the speed of marijuana,
to the apparition of Leadbelly free-styling at gunpoint.

He's rapping about the night Robert Johnson legalized the devil,
swallowing poisoned whiskey and Benjamin's Hennessy.

50 flies on, to see Big Boi and Andre, jamming
with an 808 chain gang,

hammers pounding tracks on beat,
the spectre of Rosa Parks still sending them the finger.

Dr. Dre
is burying his wife, the soil black as asphalt,
smelling like the last breath of Bessie Smith.
Dr. Dre

is crying, but he's so smooth his shaking shoulders disguise
as krumpin', face glistening with the aftermath of funk.

50 is grieving for the death of crunk,
as Lil Jon discovers he's happier

slaving in the house,
every order from the 'massa' answered by a *what* or *okay*.

In the basement is Kanye, in hiding
at an abolitionist's house and can't help

sampling the spirituals in his memory,
and all the while,

Lil Kim's baby *refuses* to come out.

I'm trying to tell you what hip-hop means to me.
This is how it sounds in my head,

when they forget to inject auto tune in our screams,
when my people believe their skin tone

is only as dark as their play list,
when they'd laugh at the very thought

of 50 Cent playing violin.

But they're not seeing John Legend,
breaking his fingers under the teachings

of Scott Joplin; Method Man building a djembe
out of his own shed skin.

That chain gang's singing Timbaland to keep on beat,
pounding those tracks 'til that train comes,

barreling from the
Underground:

Howling Wolf smoking a blunt
in the front car, dodging Eminem's spray,

roaring past that lynch mob, staring in horror...
'cause Lil Wayne

just outdid Jesus, coming back to life
still dangling from the tree. He's dropping

verses he borrowed from Johnny Cash
and Cain, his gold teeth blinding the mob's eyes;

they fall to their knees in praise of the
heaven they'd been afraid to believe.

And still, there is 50, playing so religious
he doesn't notice his own transmuting,

nine bullet wounds transfiguring,
sealed holes re-opening

Tupac stigmata. That violin
is the acoustic rage of Public Enemy,

stomping down the snake head of doubt:
Lil Kim is praying to the oncoming train.

Her baby won't come out.

Frida in Detroit

Frida.
The shadow of Henry Ford is looming over your bleeding body.
Inside that hospital, named after this man, the auto man,
the man of machine and factory, it is here
that life saw fit to steal your baby. Your second miscarriage,
another dead love in flight. But this time,
I imagine your mind: splintered, wracked, only slowly regathering
your bearings, remembering where you are: not Mexico, not
in the presence of a midwife to block the curses from your body.
You're in a hospital, in Detroit.

Frida.
I was born here. My mother delivered me in Hutzel Hospital,
and I want to believe on that morning my city was glad. Detroit and I,
we share a desire buried in our flesh: we make no promises when
you enter, but hope to be cherished when you leave.

Frida.
I grieve that your deepest memory of my city is a horror.
Your reddened sheets, your drying blood.
This is when you realized the streetcar collision had broken more
     than your back,
when you knew your body would never allow
a child to survive.

Frida.
This is my city before Motown. It is a body
that walks with no rhythm in its limp.
There is no music here but what you scrape from the concrete,
what you sweat from your back in the liver of a factory.

You lost your child here, in a land of iron and steel, where
your frantic prayers were lost without a translator.
I have known the ache of a grief you cannot explain to
those around you, as if trust were an ancient
language finally allowed to die.

Frida.
Your painting is gorgeous. While recovering from the miscarriage,
you captured your own horror, documented your agony with a
      background of factories.
I can feel why you drew this,
how at least, in your painting, you found a way to gut-punch time:
to freeze the screams splitting the mouth,
to freeze the nurse's hands,
to freeze the exodus of a crying ghost.

In your painting, you are leaving, in your *cama magica*, your magic bed,
your flying bed, you are flying back to the dirt that molded you.
You are sinking on your knees, your back to a Mayan sky,
and everything you love is sliding down,
out of the sheets,
into the dirt.

It is gorgeous. It is your right.
I only wish it did not celebrate leaving my city behind.

In your painting, I am in the background,
in the guts of an auto factory. I am looming
over you in Henry Ford's shadow.

Here is a forging of memory, irreversible,
a memorial between belly and street.
Here is a piece of a city that still weeps for you.
Here, where your faith will always have died.

HOWTOSAYGOODBYE

and this is how to say goodbye**you** make math out of your
chronicled failure steel your voice with the highest multiple of
resolveyou **stare** into the silence preparing for the words that
will pave your path out of the door**your beloved** stands beside
youbecause for you this goodbye is not to the person you've seduced
into suffering this goodbye is to the ugliest versions of you every
cell of you that transmuted a love affair into regret every **atom** of
your **tongue** that allowed such hatred to ever escape from your
mouthyour hands are a pile of trembling knucklesyou **ask** your
beloved to step aside so that you can open **your** own bellyyou are
building a heart out of a pair of **melting** hammersyour **body** is
shedding **everything that** dishonors your belovednothing is **left** but
that which has no need of forgiveness**you** love her **enough**you love
him **enough**you **give it** upyou open **up**you spill out a goodb

NATALEE

Natalee Holloway, six-and-a-half years after her kidnapping and disappearance, is officially declared dead by a judge, at the request of her father. Her mother is devastated, believing that her daughter is still alive, and will one day return.

I knew. Something told me to say
no, this is not the time, that one night
I'd open my window, to that sweet
knocking of your hands, cool and soft,
scented in dirt that would not keep you,
and I believed. I believed, at the cost
of everything one longs to call peace,
thankful. You are here, now.
I am holding you. My daughter.
Immortal. Unassailable gift of God.

Goodnight. For the last time, I'd believed
your dress'd return my girl. In dreams,
sound: the only way I'd find you. Til now,
until the kittens, sensing a presence,
mewling as if bathed in moonlight,
awaiting my haggard mind, soothing it
til shaking, groveling at a scented nothing,
my haunting, beloved. Yes, you are here.
My stolen, my ember.

Esperanza Spalding Plays Her Bass at the White House

Before she'd ever touched him, his body was being stolen
from the woods. He was being chopped and sawed,
waxed and nailed. He had not asked for this,
but grew into it, grew into the smoothed edges,
could almost forget the drum of dirt, the Yoruba of rain.
Here, Harlem zoot-suited in resin and brown, he bends to her
fingers, carries her floating soprano on his belly
to wherever she asks. But she knows: he existed well
before her hands laid claim. She's learned
how to hold his swaying frame like the hips
her mother didn't give her. Her thin fingers
rode the length of his fret wire, coaxed the thickness
from his bottom E. Here, at the White House,
mere feet from the colored man and the colored woman
bold enough to invite her Afro-ed self along
with her dark new hips, every sound he thrummed was
a letter straight to her: *the night I submitted to you,*
you promised to remember that despite our beauty
I was stolen; to remember the slices of me lovingly
glued and dried into place; to thank the woods, the dirt,
the sander, the wax, but most fervently the saw,
send thanks to the saw, for I could have never
sung for you had I not been ripped, precisely, dutifully,
quartered and scraped for the purpose of something higher.
Thank the nails, even before I can, thank the carver
for trusting my wounds to close in absolute tune.
This is what he had said, here, mere feet from the colored
man, and the colored woman,
and the girls, dear Lord the girls.

That night, as she slept, as per their arrangement,
she let him lay in the other room. Here, as her legs
slide through those starched hotel sheets, her eyelids
buzzing, a carved and hollowed frame sings as if playing itself.

He is nearly upright, leaning as if held by some lithe, phantasmic body. He sings as though he's discovered a secret of his heritage, that it is indeed possible for wood to weep, to pray to the mercy of hands.

Dear girl.
Such sleep.
Her hands.

FROM ANTONIO

Antonio Stradivari is widely considered the greatest violinmaker that has ever lived. He spent the last seventy years of his life creating over 1,100 instruments. His first wife, Francesca, died in 1698.

Francesca.
I knew you best in the woods,
where the spruce and maple waited,
dense and humming. God did not grant me a voice
to bend the heart, but rather offered the tools to build my own:
maple and spruce, a carpenter's hands and lute player's ear,
strings. Time. Thirty years of marriage taught my hands to mold
the wood into outlines of you. My violins were deliberately light,
hardly a presence in the hand; I spent my life
creating a hundred ways to render you weightless.

Every instrument I carved, shaped and varnished,
inlaid and measured, every hour of the 200 I spent on
every violin and viola and violoncello,
each held a four-count measure of what I could not say;
I hoped my callouses would translate, satisfy.

Did you notice the burn in my gaze when we attended a concert
featuring my violins? Could you hear me crackling from the bow,
stirring in the belly, shimmering in the forest's voice?
When they speak of me, a hundred years from now, their throats will
    gurgle awe
at the work of my golden period, beginning in 1698.
Francesca, did they know that this is the year you died, your legs
and laughter taken from me?

The following year I married another, but I prayed she'd
understand: a violin must be played fifty years before its true passion
    is revealed,
and Francesca, dear wife, I only had you for thirty. She was too kind
    to object,
too forgiving not to smile when I named our daughter Francesca.

I'll always love her for raising your children along with hers,
for flowing affection even when she caught your scent in my
    carpenter's dust.

Dear ghost,
if the Lord Christ had lived longer, his woodworking skill
could have been molded into music. He could have devised a blueprint
for a violin whose sound could resurrect, unearth your voice
from the belly. But to be honest, Francesca, I am still but molded dust;
to physically feel your risen voice could cause me to dissolve,

disintegrate into the workshop floor.

PAID IN FULL: A DJ'S CORONA

"Sire, only opera can do this. In a play if more than one person speaks at the same time, it's just noise, no one can understand a word. But with opera, with music... with music you can have twenty individuals all talking at the same time, and it's not noise, it's a perfect harmony!"
—*Wolfgang Mozart, in the 1983 film "Amadeus"*

The record store crates sing, *listen to me*
That collecting dust just thickens the sound
B-side of a B-side spinning you 'round
The needle's only here to set you free
Old skool, obscure, key to the recipe
Afro-ed, dashiki-ed, lookin' to get crowned
Deadened dance floors, DJs, hips all unbound
Resurrected funk is da place to be
But no, not everyone's built for the hunt
No determination to see it through
Little hunger to scratch beneath the shine
Ain't about duty, it's about the want
The record left those bite marks just for you
Our oldest prayer: *damn, that track is fine.*

> Our oldest prayer: *damn, that track is fine*
> Vinyl is the faith that you'll treat it right
> Bring it home, undress, chop it up all night
> Take a break with a cracked bottle of wine
> Strip the track of any trace of design
> First rule of ninjitsu: stay outta sight
> No time for indulgence, keep the thang tight
> Just enough drum to sharpen the bass line
> And while samples may be stuttered, brief, clipped
> While lyrics may be truncated in shout
> Precision is the mirror 'fore we drive,
> The seat belt buckle locked in at the hip
> Eric B. and Rakim shedding the doubt:
> *If I strive, then maybe I'll stay alive*

If I strive, then maybe I'll stay alive:
Away from the music, I count my days
My belly fire doused into a craze
Flirting with the ocean for a swan dive
Gripping heartbreak with bare hands in the hive
The delusional may call it a phase
Hook in the jawbone of the one that stays
Our most elegant *fuck you*'s to survive
And yes, the record is ripped pretty raw
and speakers can barely shoulder your rock
Good thing the sound man's trained to handle this
Ask him if it's too much, he'll smirk, *hell naw*
Neglected music's a feast for the clock
Only thing worse than death's an empty kiss

> *Only thing worse than death's an empty kiss*
> *Never ask the DJ to play it nice*
> *Her job is to offer the smoothest slice*
> *To make surgery the show not to miss*
> *If afterlife's the sample, make me bliss*
> *My bass line's a serpent blind from the dice*
> *My two minutes of brilliance is worth the price*
> *The splitting tongue can still manage a hiss*
> *And yet, when the listener's done dancing,*
> *he'll come hunting for me, wanting the source*
> *Needing the fullness of what I can croon*
> *This, the sound of the sample advancing*
> *This is how I can split with no remorse*
> *Good luck tasting the soup without the spoon*

Good luck tasting the soup without the spoon:
Coldcut's "Paid In Full" remix, vodka-chased
A seven-minute dish, ecstasy-laced
Homegrown ingredients ready to prune
Soul food season, a swelter none too soon
No one told me this is how rap could taste
Building a sonata from cut-n-paste
Ofra Haza soaring in Brooklyn tune
If only Israel and we could hear

this joy, heads nodding in the same room
'87 could be more than the year of my ghost
the burial of all a son holds dear
The heat of death is begun in the womb
Birth: exorcism of love from its host

> *Birth: exorcism of love from its host,*
> the dying DJ read from an old book
> not remembering from what soul he took
> it, praying less theft than leap from coast
> he sighed relief he'd never overdosed
> or let an alley grip him in its nook
> He swore he had another dish to cook
> Begged for another mp3 to post
> And yes, his last words blessing the dusted
> album, his hours in basements a grace
> his car trunk was a remix of *let there*
> *be light.* Needle: only tongue he trusted.
> The silent splicer never showed his face.
> No need when he had his music to wear.

No need when he had his music to wear,
so record store crates just sang to listen
Tell Copland and Schubert the music's real
The aria's wearing FUBU for fun
Undress the laughter and you got the steel
The track was so fine we could only stare
Composers still poor; the source is diff'rent
Just one more cut and the threading is done

Im nin 'alu/def with the record—mash
James Brown countdown, *1! 2! 3! 4!* breakin'
This is sediment built up on a dare
Snake-charming a harmony from the clash
Listen closer t'what the blacksmith's makin:
the knife, an Afro comb pierced into hair.

How to Break a Bedpost in 1960

You are a thick-boned black man
with little awareness of history.
You do not know your place in it,
feel no trace of the reverence your grand-
children will bestow you. You are only
soul and flesh. You only breathe an air
that daily wants to choke you. This
is not about heroics in the face of rope. This
is about the growling black woman in your arms,
her hungry hips, everything your tongue has been dying
to do. I mean, hell, it ain't like you was marchin' *all* the time.
Jim Crow didn't *always* feel your foot in his ass.
Your favorite nights
are not the bedtime prayers for the last friend
that was burned. It was when you and your woman
dragged yourselves to that shack, where the razor voice
of that singer was lusty supreme, the band
thumpin' in time to your grip on her ass. Her nose
burrows into your throat as the singer wails,
you dance like one body undressing itself,
seeming to say, *Hey baby, neither one of us
is dancing from a tree; lord looks like we made it again!*
When that band finally tucks the music away,
you hustle yourselves back home, ready to fuck,
not thinkin' that somewhere Malcolm X
is doin' the same thing, not thinkin' that Mahalia Jackson
is doin' the same thing, 'cause this ain't about history
but bodies, slick, colliding, and in the fourteen seconds
it takes to remove your tattered fabric, you've already
uttered your prayers: *this tongue is for you, and for our
sake I held it all day; these arms are for you, 'cause they
chose to carry more peace than fist.* And when her breasts
dove into your grateful face, every pair of Caucasian eyes
that stared her down today just caught fire, their owners
rose from their dinner tables and screamed out of
their houses, but you and your woman were too busy

to notice. 'Cause both of you know there's a purpose
to this, that you ain't nonviolent just 'cause of a Dr. King speech. It's
these bodies, this heart, this bonding that keeps you from killin' a muthafucka.
Somewhere, someone's having a dream. While you fuck.
Someone's singing they'll overcome. While you fuck. This is
my black history month. This is how I roll on *my* holiday.
This is why I smile at a black power fist; I know where those
knuckles have **been**. Before we are history, we are bodies,
collision. The right of every living mouth to lick.
Here, you are nothing of a social studies relic.
You're a starving pair of arms with a woman to grip.

CHEMO

Six years later, you remain as my lover's most exquisite
ghost, the reason she twists in our sheets, the man
who is muttered in dreams she will not remember.
You are the ex who was never mentioned
when we shared remixes of our past, the one I didn't hear
about until, naked, I touched her in the wrong spot. Two inches left
of her torso's birthmark, her voice was a haggard *stop*,
followed quickly by, *Don't worry, it isn't you.*

After she unearthed her memory of you, I understood why it'd
taken so long. But now that I know of you, now that my lover feels
        more than
ever like the soil, it's become my obsession to dig. I am a hunter,
and your scent is a distant howl from the bear trap. It's become
my fixation to remove you from every crevice in whom you
don't belong. When I'm not careful, I'm less in love than I am
in paleontology, in chemotherapy, in killing God.
I always love her best in the shower.

I write this letter as a thank you. I've never been good at
mundane. I don't know what to do with too much happy.
I love kissing with my eyes closed, so she can't feel my
foot on your grave. She doesn't need to see your calf in my
jaws. I write this knowing that this is not why she wanted
me. She never asked me to sniff out a snakebite and lick
it from her throat. I am a hunter. If I cannot wield the knife
then why was I born with it?

Some nights, she steals me away from you, in the laughter
from a silliness I'd nearly forgotten. In the kitchen,
at the stove, where water boils with no trace of your cries.
But she has learned when to avoid my gaze, reminds me
she'd already left *you* to escape a mania. I know this, and I know
she will grow tired. I write you thanks, believing that nothing I have
done can be uglier than you. I am wrong. But I won't admit this
until she leaves me. I tell myself that when she's fed up with
your scent overpowering her resilience, when she's longing

to be joy when I can only avenge her death, I tell myself
she'll know: finally, someone loved her enough to swallow you. That when
her next lover asks for her story of me, she will say, softly, *He tried.*

And when this lover finally proves himself worthy of her, when she knows
she has at last chosen wisely, she will whisper, *thank you*
for loving what is left of me. For choosing contentment
that I have survived.

GNAWED

There's something about the voice
on the other end of the line,
when I'm the one that bears the news that
our friend has died. It's the way the nothings
of the day tremor to the dirt, as the voice
gives way to the burgeoning cry,
the *No*,
the *I just saw him yesterday*,
the *Oh God*.

Looking back, there is a love in it, as if witnessing
the entire life cycle of a tiger lily in a two-minute call.
For me, it was right for us to bloom like this. It was right
for us to fall apart like this.

———

There's something about the voice
of one cut slowest by the death,
when he still reminds himself
the love of his life is not late from work.
Even now, on the phone with me,
months after her exit, at least three times
his words are swallowed in sobs.
It is his gift to grieve like this,

for losing what she had only given to him.
It was right, that months after everyone lamented
another loss and trudged on, that in one bedroom in Texas
there was still a man who lived on the verge

of splitting, that nothing would relieve the gnawing in
her last love's heart. It is right, to me, that even now

the ache is still a shock, the glistened face still fresh,
the rainmaker drawing directly from the sky.

And this is how we love. The stubborn re-enactment,
the resilience of the heart's raw.
Send us no pity. Offer any psalm you want.
Sing us anything but the words *let go*.

ABOUT THE AUTHOR

Khary Jackson is a performance poet, playwright, dancer and musician. A Detroit native, he currently resides in the Twin Cities where he serves as a teaching artist and writer. He is a Cave Canem Fellow, and as a result has further reason to adore black people. He has written 12 full length plays, one of which (*Water*) was produced in 2009 at Ink and Pulp Theatre in Chicago. He has been a recipient of several grants, including the 2010 Artist Initiative Grant for poetry from the Minnesota State Arts Board, the 2009 VERVE Spoken Word Grant from Intermedia Arts, and the Many Voices Residency from the Playwrights' Center, in 2005-06 and 2007-08. As a performance poet, he has enjoyed great success in national competition, ranking nationally in 2007, 2008 and 2009, as well as winning the National Poetry Slam with the St Paul team in 2009 and 2010. But few of us really care about all that. He's a little weird, but rest assured, there's a method to the way he stares into your house.

If You Like Khary Jackson,
Khary Jackson Likes...

New Shoes on a Dead Horse
Sierra deMulder

Racing Hummingbirds
Jeanann Verlee

Ceremony for the Choking Ghost
Karen Finneyfrock

I Love You Is Back
Derrick Brown

How to Seduce a White Boy in 10 Easy Steps
Laura Yes Yes

Write Bloody Publishing distributes and promotes great books of fiction, poetry and art every year. We are an independent press dedicated to quality literature and book design, with an office in Austin, TX.

Our employees are authors and artists so we call ourselves a family. Our design team comes from all over America: modern painters, photographers and rock album designers create book covers we're proud to be judged by.

We publish and promote 8-12 tour-savvy authors per year. We are grass-roots, D.I.Y., bootstrap believers. Pull up a good book and join the family. Support independent authors, artists and presses.

**Want to know more about Write Bloody books, authors and events?
Join our maling list at**

www.writebloody.com

WRITE BLOODY BOOKS

1,000 Black Umbrellas — Daniel McGinn

38 Bar Blues — C.R. Avery

After the Witch Hunt — Megan Falley

Aim for the Head, Zombie Anthology — Robbie Q. Telfer, editor

American Buckeye — Shappy Seasholtz

Amulet — Jason Bayani

Animal Ballistics — Sarah Morgan

Any Psalm You Want — Khary Jackson

Birthday Girl with Possum — Brendan Constantine

The Bones Below — Sierra deMulder

Born in the Year of the Butterfly Knife — Derrick C. Brown

Bring Down the Chandeliers — Tara Hardy

Ceremony for the Choking Ghost — Karen Finneyfrock

City of Insomnia — Victor D. Infante

The Constant Velocity of Trains — Lea C. Deschenes

Courage: Daring Poems for Gutsy Girls — Karen Finneyfrock, Mindy Nettifee
& Rachel McKibbens, Editors

Dear Future Boyfriend — Cristin O'Keefe Aptowicz

Don't Smell the Floss — Matty Byloos

Drunks and Other Poems of Recovery — Jack McCarthy

The Elephant Engine High Dive Revival anthology

Everything is Everything — Cristin O'Keefe Aptowicz

The Feather Room — Anis Mojgani

Gentleman Practice — Buddy Wakefield

Glitter in the Blood: A Guide to Braver Writing — Mindy Nettifee

Good Grief — Stevie Smith

The Good Things About America — Derrick Brown and Kevin Staniec, Editors

Great Balls of Flowers — Steve Abee

Hot Teen Slut — Cristin O'Keefe Aptowicz

CPSIA information can be obtained at www.ICGtesting.com
Printed in the USA
BVOW042049170313

315710BV00001B/12/P